A SMART START READER
INSECTS

Photo credits:

Cover & title page: Dwight R. Kuhn
Pages 4-5: Tom Edwards/Visuals Unlimited • Richard Walters/Visuals Unlimited
Pages 6-7: Kjell B. Sandved/Visuals Unlimited• Michael Fogden/DRK
Pages 8-9: Brian Rogers/Visuals Unlimited • Stephen J. Krasemann/DRK • Kjell B. Sandved/Visuals Unlimited • Tim Laman/Wildlife Collection
Pages 10-11: S. Callahan/Visuals Unlimited • Gustav Verderber/Visuals Unlimited
Pages 12-13: Ken Lucas/Visuals Unlimited • Kjell B. Sandved/Visuals Unlimited
Pages 14-15: Robert Calentine/Visuals Unlimited • Glenn Oliver/Visuals Unlimited • Michael Fogden/DRK
Pages 16-17: William J. Weber/Visuals Unlimited
Pages 18-19: Kjell B. Sandved/Visuals Unlimited • Leonard Lee Rue III/Visuals Unlimited
Pages 20-21: Stanley Breeden/DRK • Ken Lucas/Visuals Unlimited
Pages 22-23: Lewis Kemper/DRK
Pages 24-25: Dick Poe/Visuals Unlimited • Richard Thom/Visuals Unlimited
Pages 26-27: Fred Bruemmer/DRK
Pages 28-29: Richard Walters/Visuals Unlimited • Marty Cordano/DRK • N. H. Cheatham/DRK
Pages 30-31: John Gerlach/Visuals Unlimited • John D. Cunningham/Visuals Unlimited

No part of this publication may be reproduced in whole or in part, or stored in a retrieval system, or transmitted in any form or by any means, electronic, mechanical, photocopying, recording, or otherwise, without written permission of the publisher. For information regarding permission, write to Permissions Department, Scholastic Inc., 555 Broadway, New York, NY 10012.

ISBN 0-439-27894-5

Copyright © 2001 by Kidsbooks, Inc.
All rights reserved. Published by Scholastic Inc.
SCHOLASTIC and associated logos are trademarks and/or registered trademarks of Scholastic Inc.

12 11 10 9 8 7 6 5 4 3 2 1   1 2 3 4 5 6/0

Printed in the U.S.A.   23

First Scholastic printing, April 2001

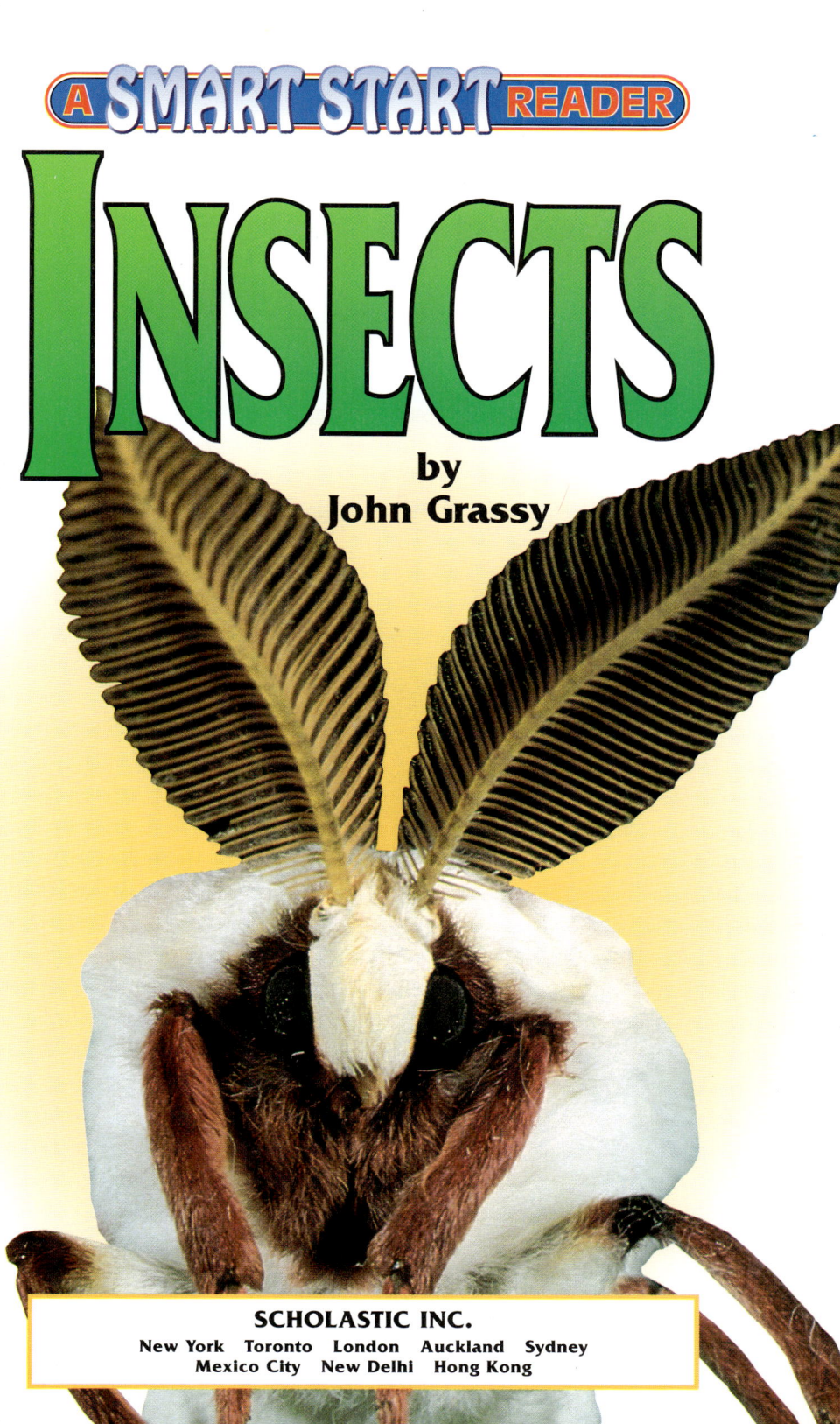

A SMART START READER

INSECTS

by
John Grassy

SCHOLASTIC INC.
New York Toronto London Auckland Sydney
Mexico City New Delhi Hong Kong

What Is an Insect?

The best way to tell an insect from other little creatures is to count legs. All insects have six legs and a hard outer covering. Spiders are not insects. They have eight legs.

◀ Dogday harvest fly

Most insects, but not all, have wings and can fly. Ants are a type of insect. Most ants have no wings and cannot fly.

Ants

So Many Insects!

Insects are all around you! They crawl on the ground, buzz in the air, and even float in the water. There are more than one million different **species,** or types, of insects. They make up the largest group of animals in the world.

▼ The eyes of a robber fly

► Glasswing butterfly

▲ Katydid

▲ Lantern bug

Beetles and More Beetles

Rhinoceros beetle

▼ Giraffe beetles

▲ Hairy weevil

There are more beetles than any other kind of insect. In fact, one in every three insects is a beetle! Many beetles can fly, and have colorful wings.

Beetles eat all kinds of things, such as other animals, dead wood, and leaves. Some beetles, known as bookworms, like to eat the paper in books!

▼ **Trilobite beetle**

Insect Life

Many insects live only a short time. They find a mate and lay eggs. Then they die. A mayfly lives only a few hours, laying its eggs on the surface of a river or lake. The cicada, however, lives for 17 years—longer than any other kind of insect.

▼ Cicada

▲ Mayfly

Eggs

How are insects born? They hatch from eggs. The eggs come in different sizes, shapes, and colors. Insects lay their eggs on leaves, in the ground, or even in the water.

The male giant water bug carries eggs on its back.

▼ Queen termite

A queen termite can lay up to 30,000 eggs each day!

Eating

Young insects eat and eat! They grow very fast.

These young grasshoppers are eating the leaves of plants.

The ant lion is a hunter. It digs a hole in the sand, like these, and hides in the bottom. When ants and other insects fall into the hole, the ant lion eats them up!

▼ Ant lion

Tricky Fellows

Many insects have tricks to help them hide from **predators.** Predators are the animals that hunt them. The tricks also help the insects sneak up on other insects. One trick is **camouflage**—

◀ Praying mantis

coloring that helps something blend in with its surroundings.

The praying mantis is a bright green color. When a praying mantis sits still, it looks just like the leaves on a tree or bush. The walking stick is an insect that looks like a branch or twig.

Walking stick ▶

Chatter Bugs

During the day, you can hear grasshoppers. They make a song by rubbing their back legs against their wings. Most kinds of insects make their own sounds. They recognize each other by the sounds they make.

▼ **Grasshopper**

▲ Cave cricket

If you go outside at night, you might hear crickets chirping. A cricket rubs its wing covers together to make that chirping sound.

Insect Cities

Some insects live in a group, or **colony.** Bees build a large nest or hive, a home for hundreds. Each bee has a job to do. Most look for food. Each colony has one queen bee. She lays all the eggs—about 2,000 a day!

Termite mounds ▲

Ants and termites live in colonies, too. A termite mound can stand 30 feet tall, with one million termites inside.

▼ A queen bee with worker bees

When Winter Comes

Some insects take a long nap all through the winter. This nap is called **hibernation.** Ladybugs and other beetles dig underground and hibernate in the soil. It may be cold and snowy out, but they stay warm and cozy in the ground.

◀ **Monarch caterpillar**

An Amazing Change

A butterfly is one of the most beautiful insects, but it starts out as a creepy, crawly caterpillar. How does it get its wings? It gets them through a special kind of change called **metamorphosis.** Hanging on to a leaf or twig, the caterpillar covers itself with a **cocoon.** The cocoon protects the animal while it changes.

Cocoon ▶

When finished, the new butterfly breaks open its cocoon and flies away.

▲ Monarch butterfly

Big Traveler

When winter comes, the monarch butterfly takes a long trip. Monarchs fly thousands of miles to escape from cold weather. This journey is called a **migration.** You would have to walk from Canada to Florida or Mexico to go as far as a monarch flies! A monarch butterfly can travel 600 miles without stopping to eat.

Monarch butterflies

What a Pest!

Some insects are real pests! Mosquitoes bite people and animals. They can spread diseases. Termites, which eat wood, cause damage to houses and trees. Grasshoppers, which eat the leaves of plants, can destroy crops that people eat.

▲ A mosquito biting human flesh

▲ Termites

▲ Grasshopper

▲ **Twelve-spot dragonfly**

Did You Know ...?

- The dragonfly is the fastest flying insect. It can reach speeds of 36 miles per hour!

- The rhinoceros beetle may be the strongest creature on Earth. It can carry up to 100 times its own weight. That is like a first-grader trying to carry a hippopotamus!

- A flea can jump 12 inches in the air. That is about the same as a person jumping 800 feet—higher than a 70-story building!

This photo of a flea has been magnified many times a flea's actual size. A flea is as tiny as the head of a pin.

Glossary

Camouflage (KAM-uh-flahj): Markings on an animal's feathers, skin, or fur that help it blend in with its surroundings.

Cocoon (kuh-KOON): The special covering that a caterpillar makes to protect itself while it goes through *metamorphosis*.

Colony (KAHL-uh-nee): A group of animals that live together and share in the work and other activities that keep the group going.

Hibernation (HY-bur-NAY-shun): A deep sleep that some animals go into during the winter, allowing them to survive low temperatures and lack of food.

Metamorphosis (MET-uh-MORE-fuh-sus): A great change in body shape, appearance, or basic structure. The change of a caterpillar into a butterfly is an example of *metamorphosis*.

Migration (my-GRAY-shun): The movement of some animals from one home to another in different places and at certain times of the year.

Predator (PRED-uh-tur): An animal that hunts and kills other animals for food.

Species (SPEE-sheez): A type of animal or plant.